Remarkable Significant Choice Discussion

Relational Abilities with Authority and Training

Carl R. Jone

TABLE OF CONTENT

INTRODUCTION

THE RIGHT WAY WHY THIS WORKS

Making the best decision in the correct manner is a major test. However, it is additionally one test that we as a whole need to prevail. Furthermore, particularly in the expert world, having the option to vanquish that challenge makes one effective.

In any case, how might you make it happen?

There are so many various ways that can prompt your objectives. Furthermore, there are countless various procedures, thus a wide range of conditions that are continually evolving.

As the change is by all accounts the main consistent, what can assist you with finding lasting success in the working environment? How might you accomplish what you need, while there are such countless choices?

As you likely have previously accepted, there is nobody with the right response. Yet, there are a few different ways that can be preferable over the others.

And negative — they are not really consistently portrayed as 'your way'.

How might you choose then?

Making the best choice

Begin with figuring out the thing is the correct thing to do. Ask yourself what are you trying to negotiate? What are your introductory reasons? What and why are you trying to follow through with commodities?

Also, what are the conceivable mid- way that can take you there? You realize that you reached the ultimate ideal when you can not any longer interrogate as to
' why' and get an alternate response. For case
" I want to admit a pay increase"(Why)
" To have farther cash"(Why)
"To manage the cost of the movements that I generally watched about"(Why)
" To learn and probe the world"(Why)
" Since I love to probe and gain some new useful knowledge."(Why)
"Since I love to learn and probe." — ultimate ideal as you can not wonder why without
chancing an alternate result, obviously what is the ultimate ideal may be different for yourself and me).

Furthermore, this is the way you find your ultimate objective, that you are attempting to accomplish with what you do. The proper thing to do is, hence, anything that brings you towards that ultimate objective.
It very well may be receiving a pay increase. Or on the other hand it may very well be finding a new line of

work that can permit you to venture to the far corners of the planet and getting compensated for it to save a similar model for above.

In any case, to sort that out, you really want to keep a receptive outlook. Ask yourself first what is your objective, and afterward settle on what the smart activity, to arrive at it, is.

How to place that practically speaking?

Ask yourself — what I'm doing now — does it finish me closer to my objective, or not?. If yes — you sorted out the thing is the correct thing to do. If not — there are many right things out there — search and find the one which is superior to what you are doing now.

Making the best choice in the correct manner

You may be making the best decision, however it doesn't work. What's more, the justification for that very well may be that there isn't the perfect opportunity yet.

Now and then prior to finishing something, it should be acknowledged in the public arena. Or on the other hand perhaps there is specialized progression required. History is brimming with such models. Leonardo da Vinci is one of them. He made such countless plans, which we as of late executed in actuality, in light of the fact that the innovation was just not prepared to place them by and by prior. Same can happen additionally to you.

What's more, this carries me to the following activity that you can do assuming you believe you are making the best decision, yet you are not obtaining the outcomes you need. Ask yourself, what is preventing you from arriving at the outcomes.

Is it perhaps that you want to accomplish something different previously? Did you perhaps miss an in the middle between? Did you as of now Member all of the means and complete all of the once propels required for the advancement of what you're doing as of now? Since — accepting that you're attempting to turn on the light in your room, it won't work expecting the light is missing.

Also, pause at that point, assuming you have your light and all the other effects you need to get there.
.Persist .
.Do whatever it takes not to give up.
.Show adaptability.

.Try more from the past.

.Give yourself time.

The world was not created overnight. Now and again we see the issues following we start doing an effort. Moreover, now and again we basically ought to be troubling and consistent and the outgrowth ends up being clear with time.

fantasize your ideal as a seed. The seed requires warmth, water, and food. In a similar manner, when it has all of that, it needs new time. A day won't make a difference. Within a few weeks or even a month, the green appearance will appear, and you will begin to observe the development. However, you ought to be patient and reliable in your molding.

Making the best decision in the correct manner.

There's something else you need to focus on to show progress. Not simply you need to settle on the slick choice flawlessly, still you believe you should do it in the right way.

Additionally, what is the importance then, at that point?

Do it. Do what should be finished. Then again perhaps break and make it dynamite. Think about business. or, once more, think about your prices. Again comparable innumerous decisions. What is further, if you feel by and by a piece frustrated, I feel you. Life, unfortunately, isn't sensitive.

There's apparently farther than one outcome to the requests you're presenting. There's no right reaction for all of us. The right way depends upon what our personality is, where we, in time we, at period of our life we are.And what we can really find as partaken influences on finishing up what's the right way is asking yourself.The way that I am residing and performing is this product what lines up with me, and with my ongoing situation? Is the way I'm working right now making me happy and making me feel satisfied?

In the event that yes — well you're finishing impacts in the best manner you know. This is awesome, and I'm so happy for you to be agreeable with yourself.

In any case,what do you feel more accustomed to? Do you have any potential to influence how you perform at any time? Could you ever change your environment? There is no right way to act, no ideal time to make it happen, and no right way to make it happen. If not, how could you change your behavior? The slick choice depends upon you, and the ideal choice depends upon the environment wherein you are. You're the individual who's the master and the watcher and student contemporaneously. It does the same, observes, and learns. Consider what could work for you. See what's working, etc. What's more, along these lines change and adapt.

What is further, this is the pathway to make a specialist life you for the most part watched about. Similarly, for what it has an effect, in like manner the pathway to make a diurnal reality you for the most part watched about.

CHAPTER 1:

THINK FIRST

How would you settle on your decisions?There are many justifications for why it may very well be challenging to settle on a choice and pick what to do in your day and life. So much to do in this brief period. In any event, when you have laid out boundaries, there is continuously something that hinders you. Consider every one of the decisions you make making you waver in making a move, alongside the feeling of dread toward disappointment or an error, bringing about tarrying. Is there a methodology - a perspective and being - that will uphold you pursuing the best decision in each circumstance? A perspective that assists you with managing emphatically and successfully with any decision you make? I accept there is. I allude to "Right Reasoning it".

The Antagonism Impediment

Assumption resembles a quiet and frequently oblivious dress practice for pushing ahead in your life. Assumption can pull you forward, or it can keep you down, leaving you hesitant. Yet, what's this assumption in light of? A significant part of the time it depends on past mix-ups, a distressing, restless or negative insight, or the continuous messages from your adversely one-sided inside voice.

The memory of a significant number of our encounters is troubled by pressure and tension that hinted at them, and afterward by the decisions of how we performed - after the occasion. The amassing of these adversely touched encounters colors assumption and makes obstruction. Independent direction is subsequently a genuine test.

What supports clear, engaged and objective direction?

We can start the help of good independent direction, by underscoring that "close to home reactivity" is something contrary to right reasoning. Profound reactivity is the point at which some feeling that gets set off by an occasion, unwittingly predispositions direction. Feelings and sentiments are a vital piece of life, however not during choices. Subsequently, it's a given that great choices require objectivity - surveying what is going on precisely for what it is, with no inclination.

The following are Nine Parts of "Right Reasoning".

1. Moving from your old inward voice and paying attention to a solid inner parent coming from adoration, acknowledgment, empathy, backing and care. Work on addressing yourself according to this point of view.

2. Choices affecting others require two parts.

a. adhering to the Brilliant Guideline - do unto others as you would have them do unto you - and

b. defining suitable and adaptable limits offsetting self-security with weakness.

3. Care and worry for the local area and offering in return, and decisions/activities that help your motivation and life meaning.

4. Consider the messages you are getting from your body. This incorporates resting when exhausted, and finding opportunity to recuperate after an unpleasant encounter.

5. Monitoring judgment and any bias that will contort independent direction, including an inclination to search for what can turn out badly, as well as a racial predisposition. Furthermore, searching for the uplifting outlook in any circumstance.

6. Not permitting dread or gloomy feelings like outrage, to impact your direction.

7. Bringing yourself completely present and centered at the time for best commitment of your prefrontal cortex during navigation. This can be worked with by a couple of full breaths, letting the air out easing back. This method turns out to be significantly more powerful whenever rehearsed.

8. Ensuring you are not caught in shut - old - thinking, and that you are using all pertinent new fair data in your direction.

9. Establishing yourself in your capabilities and capacities that assist you with connecting emphatically. What's more, coming from a point of view of overflow, not shortage.

CHARACTERIZE YOUR NEW YOU

People are looking for information about how your characteristics and attributes align with the chops they believe will succeed in the job. Include quantifiable results, if possible, to demonstrate how you use your stylish credits to achieve success.

How Should You Portray Yourself?
consider these,

I am vigorous about my work.

" Energy" evokes passions of devotion and fastness, despite the fact that every business seeks to hire people who laboriously share in their work. Right when someone is enthusiastic about the work they're doing, they're generally devoted to quality and positive issues.

" I am vivacious about my work. Since I love what I do, I've a predictable wellspring of provocation that drives me to invest some intrepid energy. In my last work, this excitement drove me to challenge myself regularly and get new capacities that helped me with achieving better work. For example, I demonstrated to myself how to modify the nature of our designs and photos using Photoshop. I in a little while converted into the primary concern of contact for any arrangement needs."

I am forceful and driven

Hankering and drive are two rates that are abecedarian for progress and advancement in numerous positions. When a company hires an aggressive contender, they can be sure that this recently hired platoon member will constantly look for ways to ameliorate themselves and remain focused on their coming thing.

" I am forceful and driven. I bloom with challenge and persistently set forth pretensions for myself, so I've got a commodity to essay towards. I do not like to settle, so I always look for amazing openings to grow and make a difference. In my once work, I was progressed on different occasions in lower than two times"

I am significantly planned.
 An systematized contender is a faithful freshman and someone a business can trust to satisfy time conditions. This quality is especially huge in executive

positions, design the board and colorful positions that anticipate that adherence should process and quality.

" I am significantly planned. I in and large take notes, and I use a movement of widgets to help myself with keeping harmonious over deadlines. In order to always be ready to find what I want, I like to maintain a perfect workspace and concoct a sensible recording strategy. I track down this accruals acceptability and besides help the rest of the gathering with staying on track. In my last work, I made one further archiving cycle that extended departmental capability by 25."

I am an gregarious person
Certain people are generally well inclined, conversational and instantly track down approaches to feeling good in social events of complete rejects.

Experts in customer backing and deals positions especially profit from this particularity.

" I am a backslapper. I enjoy getting to know new people and learning about their lives and guests . I can constantly sort out commodities that would rate settling on with rejects, and I like making people feel much better in my presence. I find this capacity is especially helpful while getting going undertakings with new guests. In my once work, my guests' purchaser unwaveringly scores were 15 over the association ordinary."

I am a trademark master

While you can show people the board capacities, certain people naturally anticipate the occupation of a precursor in friendly scenes. Directors frequently search for normal trailblazers for drive and non-managerial jobs since they set a pukka model and can lift a bunch of certainty positions.

" I am a typical commander. I've over the long haul been raised to a strategic, influential place in principally every occupation since I like to help people. I find associates naturally come to me with colorful types of review anyhow, when I am not in a crucial place of power since, assuming that I do not have indeed the outermost indication about the response, I'll unnaturally point them in the right direction. In my last two positions, I was raised to nonsupervisory jobs after a time with the association."

I am affect arranged

A result of an arranged new sprat on the block is someone who recollects a definitive thing and knows which coffers it'll take to show up. When heads hire people who are concentrated on results, they know that they will take care of business.

" I am results- acquainted, constantly checking in to determine how close or far we're from each other and what it'll take to get going. I track down this strain moving and an uncommon provocation for the rest of the gathering. Truly, throughout the span of the last time, I had the choice to help my gathering with shortening our ordinary thing time to parade by around fourteen days."

I'm a phenomenal communicator
Viable correspondence abilities are fundamental for continuous progress in practically any position and

each industry, yet they don't generally work out easily for everybody. At the point when an up-and-comer can convey well, they assist with guaranteeing messages are not obfuscated inside or while conveying data to a client.

"I'm an astounding communicator. I invest wholeheartedly in myself on ensuring individuals have the right data since it drives improved results. Most business issues originate from unfortunate correspondence, so I feel an obligation to keep everybody in total agreement. These abilities assisted with expanding my own client consistency standard by in excess of 40% in a year and assisted the group with conveying 100% of our tasks by the first cutoff time."

CHAPTER 2:

MANNER OF SPEAKING

Grasping the Essential Standards of Kindness

Great habits in correspondence are the foundation of effective business connections. Understanding the fundamental standards of graciousness in correspondence is imperative for keeping up with impressive skill and encouraging positivity.

.As a matter of some importance, undivided attention is fundamental. Focusing entirely on the individual you're speaking with exhibits regard and shows that their viewpoints and thoughts matter. It likewise assists you with completely grasping their requirements and concerns, permitting you to properly answer.

Besides, being aware of your tone and non-verbal communication can essentially affect how your message is gotten. Talking tranquilly and keeping up with open non-verbal communication conveys a feeling of congeniality and genuineness, encouraging a more useful discussion.

.Ultimately, it's essential to be aware of your language decision. Utilizing courteous and deferential language establishes an inspirational vibe for the discussion and advances a cooperative and conscious climate.

The Job and Effect of Good Habits.

In the quick moving universe of business, exchanges are occurring left and right. Bargains are made, contracts are marked, and arrangements are reached. Amidst this hustle, sitting above the significance of good habits in business correspondence in these transactions is simple.

Notwithstanding, great habits assume a critical part in building trust and believability in deals. At the point when you approach dealings and conversations with a deferential and obliging disposition, you show the other party that you esteem their time, feelings, and necessities.

This makes a positive and cooperative climate, where the two players are more ready to cooperate towards a commonly helpful result. Then again, when great habits are deficient with regards to, it can prompt stressed connections, errors, and, surprisingly, the breakdown of the whole exchange.

Great habits in deals can leave an enduring effect and set the establishment for future connections.

In an expert setting, saying "please" and "much obliged" may seem like straightforward motions, yet they hold massive worth. These little words go far in extending admiration, appreciation, and amazing skill.

At the point when you say "please," you recognize that you are making a solicitation and perceive that the other individual has the decision to satisfy it or not.

This shows a feeling of lowliness and acknowledgment of their independence. Then again, saying "much obliged" shows appreciation and recognizes the endeavors and commitments of others.

It shows that you esteem their work and the effect it has on your own prosperity. By integrating these expressions into your business correspondence, you cultivate a positive and deferential climate that supports coordinated effort, makes everyone feel better, and constructs more grounded connections.

So,remember to constantly say "please and much obliged" . The straightforward thoughtful gesture can have a tremendous effect on your expert connections.

BUILD A RELATIONSHIP THAT WILL CHANGE YOUR LIFE

As individuals were typically friendly, it's smart that the better our associations, the more euphoric we are. This applies to our personal lives as well as our workplaces: having positive relationships
with the people you interact with every day will make you feel happier, more involved, and more useful.
All positions require affiliation ultimately, so associations are crucial. There are many benefits to having strong work connections. It similarly makes going to work really beguiling.

What are the benefits?
The chief benefits of good working associations are:
  .**Extended productivity** - when people get along, they are ordinarily more helpful
  .**Further created confirmation** - you'll be generally more happy at work

.Convincing participation - extraordinary associations will decidedly impact filling in altogether

.Extraordinary for personal growth - you can benefit from the data on your partners and feel asked to win in your work

Five techniques for building strong associations

Coming up next are five top ways for laying solid areas for work.

1. Keep correspondences open and honest.

Whether it's over the phone, in person, or via email, effective correspondence is essential to building strong connections. Being open, authentic and capable spreads out trust and liking.

Listening is also basically as huge as talking. Full focus is a critical mastery to make and helps work with trusting. Consider what others have to say and give yourself time to think about it before responding.

2. Encourage relationship building capacities

This infers your ability to interface with others. Encouraging your own relationship building capacities will help you with building productive associations. For example, how you oversee battle and handle your own resources and deficiencies.

You can also deal with your deep understanding of other people, or your ability to understand what your feelings mean to you and the people around you.

3. Respecting and giving others value is a powerful way to build relationships. Put away a couple of moments for everyone, regardless of what their work - don't just focus on stunning positioning staff.

Accepting you center around something, guarantee you complete the task. Ceaselessly endeavor to satisfy time limitations and finish responsibilities or requests. Fundamentally, treat others as the need might arise to be managed.

4. Be consistent and show

your support by demonstrating your worth and demonstrating your expertise by demonstrating your time. So be proactive, help others and if there's an opportunity to assist with something - take it.

As well as introducing your own expertise, try to demand help or guidance. Generally, people are happy to offer assistance and like to feel strong so take advantage of their capacities and data.

5. Be positive

It will in general be alluring to take part in snitch and work environment issues to feel like a piece of things, yet don't take an interest. Maintain a professional attitude and address any issues.

CHAPTER 3

ACCEPT AND SUCCEED

Acknowledgment is vital to making progress, regardless of what your objectives might be. By creating self-acknowledgement, tolerating your ongoing conditions, and understanding and esteeming the viewpoints of people around you, you can establish a climate that backings and empowers your self-improvement and progress.

Regardless of what objectives you have throughout everyday life, it is essential to comprehend that acknowledgment can assume a significant part in assisting you with accomplishing them.

Despite the fact that it might appear to be nonsensical, having self-acknowledgement, acknowledgment of your ongoing conditions, and acknowledgment of people around you are fundamental advances that will put you on the way to progress.

The main sort of acknowledgment to rehearse is self-acknowledgement.

Customarily, we center such a great amount around our deepest desires and ideal dreams for our lives that we neglect to genuinely appreciate and acknowledge where we are at the present time.

.Self-acknowledgment doesn't mean you need to be satisfied with where you are — it essentially implies that you should gain and develop from your ongoing conditions.

.It's comprehension that while progress is underway, you can invest heavily in the headway that you have proactively made.

.Knowing what your identity is and what you are able to do, instead of zeroing in on what you need or what you accept you ought to be, is fundamental for fostering the interior inspiration to arrive at your objectives.

It is likewise critical to acknowledge your ongoing conditions as a spot to begin from.

Tolerating the present status of your life implies

.Being careful and perceiving the significance of exploiting the assets that are accessible to you.

It implies understanding that this is an ideal opportunity to define attainable objectives and to zero in on proactive and positive critical thinking as opposed to harping on what you have no control over.

At last, acknowledge everyone around you.

Treating everyone around you with empathy and regard will assist with building connections and give outside inspiration to achieve your objectives.Esteem the thoughts and points of view of others, search for answers for difficulties together, and perceive the up-sides of interfacing with somebody whose assessment varies from yours.

OFFER YOUR BEST ARRANGEMENT

you need further than a good — or indeed great — study. You need to be effective, flexible, and creative, and you should develop the capability to pay close attention to the small details while Norway loses sight of the big picture.

Having connections to fresh coffers can help you get started and keep it growing.

1. **gain a coordinated image:**You should in like manner be prepared to make a couple of individual retaliations. Anything kind of business you have at the loftiest point of the need list, these nine introductory hints, To gain ground as a business visionary you at first should be complete. That will help you with completing arrears gainfully and keep harmonious over the colorful effects that ought to be done. A

direct fashion for getting and staying composed is to make an arrangement for the day constantly. As you complete everything, mark it off your overview. Flash back that a couple of tasks are an advanced need than others. Mean to deal with the serious need bones first.

2. Keep Point by Point Records: Notwithstanding the way that they are involved, compelling associations put away an edge to keep up with aware records. Hence, you know where your business stands financially and can much of the time get an unexampled(and earlier) handle of any implicit challenges you might face.

3. Examine Your Resistance: To make enduring progress, you can only with significant trouble disregard your adversaries. Take advantage of some time to study and learn from them, all effects being equal. How you approach looking at the resistance can depend upon the possibility of your business. In case you are a boîte or seller, you may basically have the choice to eat or protect at a contender's business climate, ask guests what they like or could manage without it, and gain information that way. still, for case, delivering, If you are in a field with further confined authorization to your opponents' internal tasks.

4. **Handle the pitfalls and Prizes:** Another vital aspect for making progress is continuing with painstakingly counted out approaches to help your business with creating. Other than taking into account the normal awards in case you succeed, a respectable

request to present is" What is the disadvantage if this does not work out?" If you can answer that request, you will comprehend what the most over the top hopeless result possible is. You should give it a shot if you're suitable to deal with that situation and are willing to do whatever it takes to deal with the threat as much as is reasonable. Else, this could be an extraordinary occasion to contemplate different entries. Understanding pitfalls and prizes integrates being splendid about the medication of starting a business or shipping off another thing.

5. Be creative and always: look for new ways to ameliorate your business and set it piecemeal from the competition. See that you do not know everything and be accessible to vital contemplations and different procedures. Pay special attention to likely openings to develop your nonstop business or cultivate affiliated trials that will incite fresh livelihoods and give the downside of enhancement.

6. Focus on Your pretensions: The recognizable saying" Rome was not certain a day" applies to erecting a business as well. Indeed if you start a business, you will not start making plutocrats right down. It expects adventure to let people know your character and what you offer that would be useful, so stay fixed on achieving your targets. Indeed, the maturity of business possessors who make progress will not see a benefit for many times, so they will need to calculate on acquired cash(if they can get it) or their own reserve finances to support the company until it can come profitable. Fortunately, there are colorful approaches to financing a business. That being said, if the business is not bringing in cash after a reasonable time span, it is worth examining the reason why and whether the business needs to head in a different direction.

7. Give implausible customer care: similar innumerous associations neglect to recollect the meaning of giving unknown customer care.However, they'll be more arranged to come to you the coexisting time they need commodity rather of going to your resistance, If you convey better help for your guests. Amazing backing is one key to getting High ground. A couple of associations indicate this as taking a buyer driven or customer- driven approach. In actuality, in the present hyperactive-serious business terrain, association is as a rule the major segregating element among important and meaningless associations. This is where the sententia" undersell and surpass hypotheticals" comes in, and watchful business people are artful to follow it.

8. Be reliable: thickness is an abecedarian part to affect in business. To achieve true success, you need to keep doing the effects that count every day. This will produce long- term positive propensities that will help you in bringing in plutocrats over the long term and will incontinently affect satisfied guests. guests regard thickness, also.

9. Prepare to Make A couple of retaliations: Having your own business hourly requires fiscal planning more exertion than if you were working for someone differently. That can mean plutocrat operation with less energy with musketeers and family than you need to. For anyone who's determined to succeed in business, the word that there are no weekends or recesses for entrepreneurs may be true. Guaranteeing a business is surely not ideal foreveryone.However, after a veritable tone- evaluation, you finish up you are not prepared to manage it, If.

CHAPTER 4:

STEP BY STEP INSTRUCTIONS TO REMAIN FIXED ON WHAT YOU TRULY CARE ABOUT.

As an entrepreneur, you most likely frequently end up pulled in twelve distinct bearings. Therefore, with such a volume of choices to make and pressing issues every day, your center can wander endlessly further from your objectives after some time.

At the point when your timetable is stuffed, moving toward arriving at your definitive objectives consistently requires solid and reliable commitment. Obviously, keeping up with that degree of concentration beyond your endless other everyday obligations is testing.

how occupied entrepreneurs can remain fixed on arriving at their objectives while remaining consistent with their everyday responsibilities and commitments.

1. Plan Day to day Reflection

While an instinctually normal methodology might be to limit interruption, get your head down and accomplish more, faster, it's here that authority awareness drops somewhat off an arrangement with inestimable inventiveness and innovativeness. Plan contemplation practice on your day to day daily agenda. Keep in mind the force of giving over objectives and difficulties to the extraordinary space of endless knowledge.

2. Get Your Objectives On paper

Get your objectives on paper and put them in a conspicuous spot where you work. Having obviously expressed, composed objectives is strong all by itself. Placing those objectives in your view is an extraordinary method for helping yourself to remember what you need to achieve, and afterward consistently consider whether your activities are drawing you nearer to your objectives.

3. Begin A Responsibility Club

Individuals from the club can be companions, family or other entrepreneurs hoping to keep fixed on their objectives. Relegate a turning mediator job. Gatherings ought to be held month to month, and all individuals should introduce their advancement reports on the activity plans they created toward the finish of the earlier month. Not having any desire to dishearten the gathering is a positive wellspring of tension.

4. Watch out for The Higher perspective

Move forward to the commander's room separate from the noise and distractions to appreciate the situation of where your business presently is, possibilities for where it could head and what path you really want to set to show up there. You should continuously remain no less than one stage (preferably, some more) in front of anything your ongoing exercises are to guarantee future supportability. Time and again proprietors don't contemplate the pipeline until they frantically need it.

5. See What You're Not Doing

Proprietors normally mistake their work for their venture. As a bustling proprietor, you should continually continue asking yourself, "Is this something I could need my Chief doing? Could this be the best utilization of their time?" In the event that the response is "no," the subsequent inquiry is, "On the off chance that I am doing this, what am I not doing?"

6. Assign Time For Arranging Every Week

Saving assigned arranging time every week is a significant custom for gaining ground toward any objective. The way to make this successful, however, is to audit last week first. What might you at some point celebrate? What did you realize? Also, where did you think of yourself as stuck? Knowing that, what three errands might you at some point scratch off this week that could get you rolling forward once more? Record it on paper. Plan it. Do it.

7. Lay out Clear Objectives For Various Timetables

Ensure you have a 10-year objective, a 3 HAG (three-year profoundly feasible objective) and a first concern for the year, the quarter, the month, the week and the day. To keep on track day to day, I suggest and utilize the Ivy Lee Technique: Consistently, before you finish the day, record your main six needs for the following day. Begin the day with No. 1 and follow the rundown. Toward the finish of that day, rehash it. Basic and centered!

8. Quit Performing multiple tasks

Keeping away from the compulsion to perform various tasks is one method for remaining on track. Large numbers of us figure we can perform various tasks, however we truly can't. Research upholds the way that we can zero in on each thing in turn. Remaining fixed on each thing in turn prior to moving to the following is the most ideal way to keep fixed on your objectives.

9. Start off Promptly Toward the beginning of the day

Creating calm time into your timetable to survey your day, ponder objectives and make vital arrangements can help you in zeroing in on the components that can truly have an effect in your business. What's more, before the pandemic, I utilized my driving opportunity to get clear on many issues and make arrangements for what's to come. I'll rehash that sooner rather than later, I'm certain!

10. Share Your Objectives With Others

Record them on paper and offer them to everyone. On the off chance that your guidelines of direct and objectives are straightforward to all, individuals don't need to think about what their piece of the higher perspective ought to be. They ought to know that, in every little undertaking, there is a concentration and a reason more noteworthy than their part in pursuing those objectives. Making motivations for all as you arrive at those objectives is an additional gift for groups.

11. Adhere to The Five-Minute Guideline

Each day, sit with your viewpoints, objectives and desires for five minutes. Make a dream to see yourself strolling toward them. Advise yourself that each achievement is a stage toward those objectives, and the troublesome days are groundwork for the festival. On the off chance that you can't do this each day, attempt it one time per week. Understanding what you are walking toward will keep you on target.

12. Center Around The Drawn out Methodology

Having the vision and returning to it is critical to keeping on track. Time and again entrepreneurs get occupied by momentary objectives without contemplating the drawn out methodologies that will assist with intensifying their endeavors. To remain on track, imagine and think about the first expectation of the business, clear your future with this acknowledgment and propel yourself forward.

RECOGNISE THE POSITIVE

This is an inquiry presented by organizations from one side of the planet to the other. Positive acknowledgment can be a main thrust behind representative inspiration when utilized accurately and genuinely. Basically nobody can oppose being informed that the work they set forth is valued.

In numerous ways, business has moved a long way past the days in which a check was the essential image of affirmation and appreciation for workers. An undeniably aggressive work environment implies that besides the fact that organizations seek clients, they additionally go after representatives. Regardless of how extraordinary your advantages bundle is, in the event that your workers don't feel appreciated, they might continue on toward a situation with another business.

Perceiving and Compensating Positive Ways of behaving

Spurring your representatives to take care of their best responsibilities can be a sensitive dance, especially with regards to perceiving their endeavors. To an extreme and you seem to be deceitful. Excessively little and you will be considered to be brutal. Finding some kind of harmony takes a goal.

Uplifting feedback includes perceiving and compensating wanted ways of behaving to energize their continuation. This can incorporate recognition, motivations, appreciation, or a mix of any of these activities.

Acknowledgment and award of wanted ways of behaving can affect work environment culture in numerous ways:

.Further developed confidence

.Expanded feeling of worker self-esteem and certainty

.Expanded appropriate conduct

.More noteworthy worker efficiency

.Further developed association between colleagues

.More grounded relational connections

.Expanded obligation to organization

.Further developed worker inspiration

Sounds perfect, isn't that so? What business couldn't need that? Luckily, you can set your representatives on a way to more noteworthy inspiration and efficiency with explicit commendation.

Conduct Explicit Commendation

Conduct explicit commendation is a well known uplifting feedback strategy in the instructive circle. Consolation in this configuration has been displayed to build an understudy's social and scholastic exhibition, especially for understudies with difficulties. Along these lines, encouraging feedback can decisively change the school environment and work on the instructive experience for everybody. In the working environment, conducting explicit applause can possibly make better private connections and decidedly influence representative inspiration.

Yet, how does conducting explicit acclaim work?

At the point when you use conduct explicit commendation, you let your representatives in on what you esteem in the work environment and how they show those qualities. It very well may be an immense lift to work environment feeling of confidence.

Instructions to Give Positive Acclaim and Acknowledgment

Encouraging feedback in the working environment is a powerful method for making a positive work environment culture and it expects next to zero cost. It expands your representatives' self-esteem and adds worth and possession to work execution. These characteristics can increase efficiency. Commending or applauding a representative in this manner can likewise mitigate any self-uncertainty on work execution. It is significant, notwithstanding, to get things done as needs be. Observe these rules:

Give acclaim right away: following the activity or it loses meaning.

Trustworthiness is the smartest strategy: At the point when the acclaim is earnest and sensible it implies more to the beneficiary.

Timing is everything: Build up the positive outcomes quickly following the activity.

Customize the recognition: Every representative answers diversely to acknowledgment. Know your representatives and design your acknowledgment so it delivers the best effect for every person.

Irregular, unscheduled acknowledgment: inspires more than planned acknowledgment. Successive and irregular is superior to customary, planned acknowledgment.

CHAPTER 5:

THE MOST EFFECTIVE METHOD TO BE CERTAIN YOU HOLD THE RIGHT

Similarly as we want social associations in our own lives, we likewise need to have great relations with our friends at work.

Organizing is a significant piece of vocation advancement. Also, having companions at work is significant for your social prosperity.

Yet, for a few of us, that is not exactly simple or easy.

It tends to be threatening to begin addressing another person. Quit worrying about warming up to them.

A straightforward "Hi" is sufficiently simple to connect. However at that point you want to know how to make all the difference for a discussion.

To assist you with building those significant associations, this is the way to convey a discussion like a genius.

What makes a decent discussion?

An incredible discussion consists of a few variables. Here are a portion of those perspectives which can keep those abnormal quiets under control.

1 Undivided attention:

Undivided attention is a sort of listening where the emphasis is on truly focusing while the other individual is talking. Now and again individuals pay attention to answer as opposed to standing by listening to what their discussion accomplice is talking about.

This significant listening expertise allows your discussion to accomplish realizing that you are focusing. It is an indication of the capacity to understand people on a profound level. In addition, you're bound to recall a greater amount of the discussion subsequently.

You can work on your undivided attention by echoing what you have quite recently heard once again to the speaker. Also, by doing a better job listening.

2. Posing and addressing inquiries:

One more approach to showing that you are a decent audience is to clarify some things.

Follow-up questions connected with what the other individual said can grow the discussion. Or on the other hand you can get some information about something you didn't totally have the foggiest idea or are keen on diving more deeply into.

Once more, this shows the individual you are conversing with that you are really inspired by what they need to say.

3.Tracking down shared interests and similitudes:

While having a discussion, keep your ears open for encounters that you share practically speaking. Shared interests can give you something to discuss and will keep the discussion streaming normally.

Finding similarities will likewise assist with laying out shared belief and make for a seriously compensating discussion. This is a critical consideration of how to move objective discussion along easily.

4. Having a goal for the discussion:

Whether you've chanced upon a collaborator at the store or you're having a discussion at a systems administration occasion, having an objective as a primary concern for the conversation is in every case great. Having a reasonable goal guarantees the discussion has course and isn't awkward or off-kilter.

PROFOUND DISCONNECTORS

The territory of Withdrawal:

The impacts of withdrawal can be felt in:

.your capacity to draw in and recruit extraordinary representatives

.intentional and compulsory turnover

.stress and nervousness incurred for friends and administrators

.your shopper image

.consumer loyalty

The effect of withdrawal on business.

There are different degrees and meanings of separation:

Separation as "a pessimistic, unfulfilling, business related perspective that is described by betrayal and unfaithfulness," and furthermore "the pulling out or safeguarding of oneself genuinely, intellectually, or sincerely during work job execution".

Powers of Separation:

1. Misalignment with job: Nothing can make a fresh recruit harsh quicker than finding they're not a decent counterpart for their work. Almost half (46%) of recently recruited workers bomb in 18 months or less. Just 19% accomplish what can be viewed as a straight-up progress.

Frequently, existing representatives wallow in jobs that weren't characterized enough or haven't advanced to fit the changing necessities of the business.

Work fit is a critical supporter of representative commitment and efficiency. Work fit is feeling like you're ready to be useful and fulfilled in your work and inside your organization culture. At the point when we recruit somebody whose conduct characteristics are not matched to the job, we incidentally put them in a position to fall flat. For instance, on the off chance that somebody likes to work heads down, that individual would be hopeless in a job. The entire day they'd stretch to be more social and active.

It's feasible to prepare and mentor representatives to foster new abilities. However it's desirable to search out representatives whose normal social drives fit a job well in any case. Here's the reason: Despite the fact that you can show individuals deals procedures and regardless of whether they can effectively finish on that doesn't mean they'll partake in the work or take fulfillment from their achievements. Furthermore, in the event that they aren't getting that adrenaline rush from progress, they won't feel commitment.

Frequently, existing representatives fumble in jobs that weren't characterized enough — or haven't advanced to fit the changing requirements of the business.

2. Misalignment with supervisor:

The relationship one has with their immediate chief is a basic supporter of representative commitment. As per Gallup, only 21% of representatives emphatically concur that their presentation is overseen in a manner that spurs them to accomplish exceptional work. Most directors are not outfitted with the instruction and data they need to really make due. Most have no clue about how to approach training and moving representatives.

In our kin The executives, we saw areas of strength for a between how workers feel about their directors and their mentality toward their positions. As a matter of fact, as per that report, "94% of representatives with extraordinary managers have enthusiasm and energy for their positions, though just 59% of workers with terrible supervisors have energy and energy for their positions"

3. Misalignment with group:

97% of representatives accept an absence of arrangement in a group that influences project results. Another 86% fault work environment disappointments in absence of joint effort and incapable correspondence. Furthermore, 75% of businesses rate cooperation and coordinated effort as "vital," yet just 18% make correspondence assessments part of the execution of the board. This is significant on the grounds that organizations that don't advance and empower cooperation are more averse to high-performing.

How might you make a more adjusted group? Acquaint workers with their friends' correspondence styles and objectives. Make a point to adjust everybody on a common vision for the group as well as organization objectives and values. Individuals who are paddling in a similar course and see each other's assets are less inclined to encounter unfortunate struggle.

4. Misalignment with culture:

At the point when workers are skewed with their corporate culture, they miss the mark on the sensation of having a place. This can influence execution. Absence of arrangement could in fact establish a harmful climate across the association. This can be essentially as straightforward as not feeling in line with organization values, feeling an absence of significance and reason, or having an absence of confidence in organization authority. Yet, it can likewise be a significant separate sensation of confinement and dejection, which can prompt withdrawal.

Tutoring, training, and recruiting workers in associates can assist you with building kinship, support, and social arrangement. There are likewise different ways of building an invigorated and useful culture from acquainting a common jargon with giving representatives the instruments to comprehend themselves and their colleagues better.

The most effective method to assemble commitment:

Commitment is a person's close to home obligation to their association and its objectives. Commitment is powered by fit and fulfillment with one's work, chief, association, and colleagues, and it appears as an optional exertion at work. Optional exertion is blowing away the least work necessities.

commitment comes from being tested to propel yourself and succeeding. Assuming that a worker faces a snag and the chief moves heaven and earth to make the impediment considerably less testing, the representative will not get a lot of achievement from progress. Then again, assuming that the supervisor sets the bar high and guarantees the representative has the required apparatuses and information to succeed, the worker will feel energized when they really do succeed — on the grounds that they were responsible for the outcome.

You should likewise guarantee the accompanying:

1. Work fit.

One basic part of commitment is work individual fit. Assuming you're recruiting, you'll need to direct conduct and mental evaluations to guarantee the competitor is appropriate to the job. (Being in some unacceptable occupation is like composition with your non-predominant hand for eight hours every day, five days per week.)

For representatives, offer testing, significant, and feasible work, and afterward recognize accomplishment to drive a more elevated level of commitment. You'll likewise need to rethink any work that has developed after some time to address business issues. The worker in the job could as of now not be an extraordinary fit. You ought to distinguish and address this as right off the bat as conceivable before the representative separates.

2. Supervisor arrangement.

Supervisor worker connections are regularly referred to as quite possibly the main consideration of representative commitment. Give chiefs instruments and prepare to grasp, backing, and challenge every one of their representatives. Consider having each worker take a conduct evaluation and giving chiefs admittance to modified training guides so they can mentor and guide representatives in a way that will be best.Supervisors should likewise chip away at being mindful. They can request input, take a test, or utilize a Supervisor Improvement Diagram that distinguishes weak spots and gives noteworthy hints.

3. Group elements.

Indeed, even all that chief can't generally address group misalignment. Feeling esteemed, involved, and regarded in a group is basic. Cultivate connections by providing representatives with a more profound comprehension of each other's drives, requirements, and correspondence styles. Ensure pioneers are likewise educated and delicate to group synthesis and elements — Collaboration Styles is a helpful instrument to find and fill holes in a group.

You'll likewise need to construct a different group so you can profit from a wide assortment of abilities and experience. The best chiefs comprehend that they don't have to know it all — they need to encircle themselves with a different group and draw on their consolidated information.

4. Culture arrangement.

Each time we bring some unacceptable individuals into our way of life we shift that culture further from where we need to be. Terrible recruits — regardless of how talented — won't ever flourish, and will typically make harmfulness develop. Terrible recruits are your quiet executioners (low commitment, low performing) and your polluters (low commitment, low performing).

Take care to construct an agreeable culture. Do visit worker commitment studies and really focus on the input you get from your superior workers. Find opportunity to create and impart your main goal and fabricate a worker commitment technique helpfully. Lay out and experience your qualities, and bring your kin into arrangement around them.

CHAPTER 6:

HOW TO DEAL WITH THOSE WHO TAKE CREDIT

There's nothing seriously bothering, particularly expertly, when a partner assumes praise for your diligent effort and thoughts.

Take a full breath and think about the accompanying reaction.

1. Recognize your own sentiments about the circumstance: This is fundamental in light of the fact that albeit many individuals attempt and keep away from sentiments and feelings at work, maybe thinking it makes them amateurish, sentiments really guide our activities. For this situation, your sentiments might go from somewhat disturbed to blazingly enraged. At the point when you set aside some margin to enlist your sentiments they quite often die down in power, which leaves you better ready to ponder what is happening.

2. Presently, consider these sentiments and the circumstance: give yourself an opportunity to truly think as opposed to just responding. Consider the reason why the circumstance could have happened:

• Was it essentially an oversight?

• A mistake?

• Was it purposeful, to acquire praise?

• Or on the other hand was it malignant, to sabotage you?

A pen and paper, having an espresso away from the climate or taking a walk can assist you with managing this interaction. There might be many reasons or only one - you might very well never know the genuine response. However, the key is utilizing this chance to mull over your choices.

3. Figure out what move to initiate: Sound connections require solid however direct correspondence. Carve out an opportunity to raise the issue with your partner. Try not to utilize fault. Rather, lounge chair your concern regarding a difficulty and use "I" explanations (as opposed to "you"). Make sense of what result you are searching for. This habitually works and can be utilized to construct a functioning relationship. On the off chance that you suspect your remarks will fail to receive any notice, have a third

individual present who will keep you both "legitimate" in the discussion and forestall matters deteriorating.

STANDARDS MAINTENANCE

How would you keep your upkeep program on target and yield the best outcomes from your speculation? These six standards will help:

1. Plan, as opposed to respond: Center assets around forestalling margin time, not on responding to margin time you ought to have forestalled. At the point when there's disappointment, decide the reason and sort out some way to forestall that cause proceeding. For instance, engines in the competing region flop habitually. The reason is a dissolvable engine that helps into the windings through the engine vents — so catch and fumes the dissolvable, or utilize completely encased engines.

2. Be prepared to finish the work: Figuring you can do the best occupation without the best test gear, instruments, and preparing is living in fantasy land. Figuring you can finish any work securely while holding back on wellbeing preparing, PPE, and an (nearly) fanatical wellbeing society is hazardous reasoning.

3. Stick to the script: An arrangement won't work in the event that you don't follow it. Without a doubt, you might have to change it and make an incidental special case as extraordinary conditions (and good judgment!) may direct. In any case, don't wander from the arrangement since somebody in activities or the board shouts noisily enough. Continuously make sense of the arrangement, and in the event that somebody needs an exemption, have them present a legitimate defense for it. For instance, all the support for Line 3 is in the CMMS and booked for a considerable length of time from now. However, one month from now, this line is being tapped to take care of enormous requests and activities and maintains that you should do all the PM work now rather than when runtime is so basic. There is just a single right response and "we're staying on track" isn't it.

4. Effectively look for criticism and counsel: This is a difficult situation, and you can't know it all! Indeed, obviously get input from administrators and upkeep individuals, yet work out positively past your nearby environmental elements. Great sources incorporate industry distributions, industry gatherings, industry guidelines, courses, studios, homeroom preparing, reference guides, and companions that you network with through industry associations.

5. Change depending on the situation: Getting all that criticism and counsel is inconsequential in the event that you don't utilize it when it might have an effect.

6. Keep others in the know: Try not to simply change something "in the administrative center." Convey changes and unique exercises to the individuals who might be impacted. For instance, you could email the pertinent division heads and bosses that you're leading both a thermographic review and a power investigation on Region X next Thursday, rather than simply the typical voltage checks. Then, at that point, share with them your discoveries (simply be compact). They will value being kept in the know, and you're exhibiting the way that support is keeping steady over things.

CONCLUSION

Remarkable SignificantChoice Discussion:"Relational Abilities with Authority and Training", perusers leave on an intoxicating bid to open the privileged perceptivity of significant independent direction. Digging into the core of life changing opinions, this arresting story enlightens the significant impact of our choices on our excursions, moving people to regulate the craft of decision for individual and aggregate advancement.This story entices compendiums to come masters of their fates by weaving a web of touching narratives, practical advice, and amping strategies.

It's a song of devotion to the strength and limit inside every existent to shape purposeful, significant, and groundbreaking ways through conscious decision. " Remarkable Significant Choice Discussion" is a must-see experience that combines the cinematic beauty of liars with the amping power of practicable perceptivity. It's a passage of extending implicit and untapped capabilities.

At its center, this story fills in as an assignment to battle, empowering perusers to leave on a instigative odyssey of tone- strengthening, striking versatility, and shrewd navigation. It remains as a satisfying demonstration of the unbounded likely epitomized inside each choice, soliciting people to hold onto the arm of their predeterminations and realize unknown, life changing changes.

"Remarkable Significant Choice Discussion" in conclusion Relational Abilities with Authority and Training" is an extraordinary exposure, a call to regard the important murmurs of decision, and change them into resonating reverberations of significant effect. It remains as an unfaltering signal, encouraging perusers to embrace their association, shape fates, and engrave endless birthrights through the significant craft of decision.

Leave on the excursion of groundbreaking decision, enlighten your way to significance, and content an eventual fate of measureless chance with" Remarkable Significant Choice Discussion:Relational Abilities with Authority and Training" moment.